FROM CITY TO VALLEY

The War Children.

Chris Andrews

ISBN: 978-1-7394575-2-5 (paperback)
ISBN: 978-1-7394575-0-1 (hardback)
ISBN: 978-1-7394575-1-8 (eBook)

From City to Valley: The War Children copyright © 2023 Chris Andrews
All illustrations © 2023 Nikki Davies

Chris Andrews asserts the right to be identified as the author of this work in accordance with the Copyright Designs and Patents Act 1988. All rights reserved.

No part of this publication can be reproduced or transmitted in any form or by any means, electronic, mechanical or otherwise, without the express written permission of Chris Andrews.

All characters appearing in this work are fictitious. Any resemblance to real persons, living or dead, is purely coincidental.

CONTENTS

PREFACE.
ONE WORD. 1
JOURNEY. 7
DEFINING NAUGHTY. 13
ROOM. 17
DIARY. 25
INVITATION. 31
SEARCHING. 37
SARAH. 43
DEAR MUM. 47
HERE BE DRAGONS. 53
HAPPINESS. 59
GOODBYES. 63
ACKNOWLEDGEMENTS.
ABOUT THE AUTHOR.

This book is dedicated to my daughter; for her encouragement, assistance, and forbearance.

And for Peter, who believed.

PREFACE.

Dear Reader,

You may be wondering why, all this time after the two World Wars, at my need to write the stories of London children evacuated away from home and the people they loved to an unknown land. The relevance is this - these children were literally cast adrift from the anchor of home; for their own safety admittedly, from war-ravaged London and all they had ever known.

They were children without their loving parent, or protecting adult keeping watch over them; they were vulnerable. I feel so strongly that we all have a responsibility for the wellbeing of every child; so many children still needing protection, and sadly that this will probably always be so. It applies today just as much as it did in any other day or time, and any raising of that consciousness can only help. Part of my working life was with families of every permutation, who had children damaged in many ways, and were needing help and care. Raising awareness and communal responsibility is therefore a purpose close to my heart.

This series of voices arrived in my head unsought and unexpected. The boy 'Billy' came first. He was the result of a Writers Group topic titled 'Defining Naughty', for which I wrote several pieces. Where did he come from? I have no idea, but he was very real, with a face, a voice, a past and hopefully a future. And he was a child alone, far from home.

Other voices began to arrive. The first World War nurse, so near and clear to me, had a chance meeting that affected the life direction of the person who became a Primary School teacher in the East End. The teacher who took her young pupils away from the Blitz to another country and had to leave them there in trust.

The voices kept coming; their stories interlocking and taking over until they were writing themselves.

Thinking about the children who were evacuated from the East End of London (my birthplace) leaving their parents and families behind on the station platform at Paddington, most not understanding that it wasn't going to be a day out, or a little holiday, but a long time in the houses of strangers; these thoughts let me into their world.

Talking to my cousin later, I discovered she and her younger sister had been suffering from TB immediately after the war and were sent away to a sanatorium in the country. She remembered the anguish of saying goodbye to her parents at the big iron gates on visiting days, wondering if they would forget where she was. She had written home regularly, and amazingly her letters were kept. She allowed me to read and use them. They were so touching and poignant and gave such insight into how it felt to be one of those exiled children. She and her sister were away for half a year, and I wondered if the children who experienced a two or three-year absence from their families ever fully recovered from that forced separation. From a child's point of view, the bottom-line feeling must always be: 'You left me'. Rejection.

I doubt anyone involved in caring for evacuee children was unaffected by their presence. Some children struck lucky, others didn't. I've spoken to a number of people who had the experience as children in different parts of the country; for many it was the best time of their lives. Food, freedom and fresh air as opposed to the city streets, bombsite playgrounds and food rationing that they returned to. We will never know the unrecorded extent of the unhappiness of others.

My illustrator Nikki Davies was one of several young artists suggested to me for this project: her work stood out, with a simple charm, and a look just right for my voices. She seemed quickly to tune in to how I was seeing them. This is what Nikki says of herself:

'My sister started me painting when I was young and bought me my first watercolour set. I enjoyed being read to, and loved the illustrations of Shirley Hughes and Janet Ahlberg, who have probably inspired my style. I went on to take a Foundation Degree in Fine Arts.

I am an Autistic illustrator, and I began drawing people and the exchanges between them from a very young age. It helped me gain a deeper understanding of emotion in faces, and how to be in this world where the thing that unites us all is how we relate to one another. Growing up in rural Bedfordshire inspired a love of nature and animals which I enjoy including in my work.

Art became my joy and my therapy, and I use it often to gift my friends.'

My grateful thanks go to Nikki, for giving life to my voices.

And I will now let the voices speak for themselves.

ONE WORD.

1914

Sitting here in the last of the afternoon sun, they are, a couple of dozen of them; some in Bath-chairs, some we've pushed out onto the terrace in their beds and a few who've walked out on their crutches and damaged limbs. I walk amongst them, tucking in rugs, doing up a button or two, touching a hand, whilst answering back a bit of cheeky repartee. They don't lose that, these boys. Keeps us all going. I feel a right Florence sometimes, bit of a fraud in a way; what do I know about nursing?

Of course, I could have said no, when the Authorities asked me if I'd volunteer for nursing the wounded, or would I rather go to the Munitions factory? Well, then I asked where I'd be posted to if I went nursing, and they said, Deal, on the Kent coast; I heard my voice saying a firm yes. I got to thinking, that well, I could probably do nursing. Growing up in Hackney, you see plenty of the seamier side of life, and helping Dad in the shop, butchering, means I've never been a girl to faint away at the sight of blood. Five sisters, I've got, and Dad with no sons, taught us all to work in the business and grow up strong and practical.

The other thing was, they said Deal was on the coast, which meant I'd be near the sea. I'd only seen it once, when we had a Sunday School outing and went on the steam train from Liverpool Street to Southend, getting told off for letting down the leather strap to open the windows, and leaning out, and getting smuts in our eyes. Ten, I was then, and when we got down the front and on the beach, I can still feel myself standing barefoot with the muddy sand squelching up between my toes; overawed by the sight of all that water and how it sparkled, and wondering where it ended.

So here I am in my uniform, doing my bit for the War effort, taking care of my poor boys, and able to look out every day from the windows of this big old house, down the long green field of the lawn to the ocean. Sometimes I get an hour off, and I go down the cliff path, mesmerised and drawn by the sound of the water. I take my boots off and just stand there, with my feet in the surf, breathing in freedom, and feeling my whole straight body all alive. Most of my wounded boys will never do that again. So, I do it for them, taking lungfuls of salty air, as though I could breathe it into them.

Night duty is perhaps the worst, or the best, depending on how you look at it. At night the terrors and nightmare memories seem to take hold of them, in the dark; no surprise really, and we go from bed to bed with a lantern, soothing with a touch, giving water and help for their pain if we can. Waking them gently if they are screaming in their sleep. Don't know how many times I've got engaged doing this. Some poor lad will say, Nurse, will you marry me, when I get out of here? I never met an angel before.

So, I say yes, of course I will, knowing sometimes that the poor boy probably won't see the morning. Then in that moment when they smile at me in the lamplight, because I've said yes, I feel I've done something worthwhile. Such a simple little word, giving such happiness, even though they know you don't really mean it.

The last of the afternoon sunlight is going, and we start to wheel them back into their wards. The trees are changing colour, it's the start of Autumn, and the Poplars are casting long shadows across the grass. London's full of Poplars, that's how I know what they are. Dad used to take us up Victoria Park on a Sunday and show us the trees, and say this poem, "The Poplars in the fields of France are golden ladies come to dance". I didn't think I was listening, but I must have been. The boys over there won't be seeing any golden ladies for a while yet. The sea is navy blue today. Hark at me! Getting quite poetical! There's a chap who reads us poems sometimes after tea, that his friend wrote in the trenches. The friend died; got gassed, so he brought his notebook back. They're a bit sad, the poems, but they make you feel all stirred up inside, about what's right and what's wrong. This is wrong, all these young men killing each other for no good reason.

We hear the waves breaking on the shore, and the squawk of the gulls. Mewing they call it, like cats do. Across that water, I think, is France and Flanders, and our boys are there in their trenches; stinking, wet, bitten by fleas, eating rats to stretch the rations. Not much glory, as far as I can make out. They say it'll go on for another year yet.

And it seems to me, that the only glory and winning would be, if everyone, the Germans too, the Officers and all of them, stood up and climbed out of their trenches and said, No, we're not doing this any longer, and walked off to go home.

Just for a moment I'm lost in this beautiful dream where there is no more war, no more killing or mutilated bodies.

Then reality jerks me back as I hear the familiar chug of the Motor Ambulance heading up the drive. I straighten my cap and my shoulders, and go to meet it. No is not an option. And I wouldn't say it if it were.

JOURNEY.

1940

No, please, do open the window; it's a long ride from here to Paddington. Five hours, if we don't get held up, the Guard said. Jolly muggy day, isn't it? This rain! You wouldn't think there could be any more water in the sky. Grey. Can't see the hills.

The children are going to get wet feet, all of them with only the boots and shoes they stood up in. Most of those outworn or outgrown too. Poor little feet. I've got to toughen up, I've done my duty. Got them here to safety, away from the Blitz.

Oh, thank you, that is kind, I seem to have mislaid my hanky. Smuts in my eyes. No, that isn't true, leaving my pupils here, with strangers, in the unknown. Many of them didn't even know where Wales was, until we looked at my Atlas on the train. One of the little ones was really worried that it was something to do with Jonah and the whale, and thought he was on his way to get swallowed.

Are you travelling all the way to London? Nursing? How wonderful. Joining up for the War effort. To make a difference.

I met a wartime nurse once, the Great War of course. She was an East End girl, nursed my Arthur at the end, that's why she wrote to me. He was my fiancée, we didn't have the chance to marry, before he. She was at the field hospital in Deal, where they took him after the Somme, he'd lost a leg you see. She wanted to tell me how brave he'd been, and how he'd talked about me. I met her at Marble Arch, in the Lyon's Corner House, after the War. I think she'd taken a bit of a shine to my Arthur, not surprising, he was a lovely chap, could charm the birds off the trees. She said even with the pain he had to bear; he would try to cheer everyone up. Hobbling around on his crutches, having a chat here and there, in the evening, often, when the other chaps were generally pretty low. Three months he lasted, before the gangrene set in. They did their best for him.

She was a Butcher's daughter, from the East End of London, big strong girl, with a heart as big as a football. She sought me out to tell me how he'd been, and oh yes, it helped. The not knowing was worse.

She was the reason I took a teaching post in Bethnal Green, I wanted to make a difference too, if I could, to children like her.

No, I grew up in Surrey, boarding school and all that. Daddy was in the Foreign Office, away a lot. I missed Mummy and my pony and the dogs dreadfully when I was away at school. My parents were quite radical in their thinking for the times, believed in education, even though I was an only child, and a girl. My Grandmother was quite horrified that I wasn't going to do a 'season' and get presented and be trotted out for the marriage market, like a show pony. Didn't think it quite decent for a girl to pursue a career, especially teaching. She never quite forgave my parents for that. Not that they could have stopped me, even if they'd wanted to. I'd set my course.

Do you have a sweetheart? What a pretty ring! The Welsh Guards? Very fitting. No, never anyone else for me after my Arthur.

My pupils are as precious to me as our own children would have been. I'm sorry, I'm so emotional, I don't know why I'm finding leaving them behind so hard. I've made a mess of your hanky. Terribly kind of you, thank you.

Some of them touch your heart more than others. One little lad had to be separated from his big sister. They took her on the Farm, but wouldn't have him. Dear little chap. Big brown eyes and freckles across his nose. Only seven. Was distraught when his sister left him, turned white as a ghost, too brave to cry. I had to leave him at the Manse, the big house, with the Minister and his wife. They didn't want him, or any child, but the Welfare woman insisted, all those empty rooms. I hope he'll be alright. No children of their own. Man of the Church. I must stop worrying.

His sister will be, I'm sure, got her head screwed on, that one. She'll watch out for her little brother.

Then there were the twins. Peas in a pod. The Bobbsey twins, I called them, did you read those stories as a child? My class love them, Friday afternoon Storytime. Sitting crossed legged on the wooden floor of the school hall, the sun coming through the windows and lighting up the picture of the Laughing Cavalier on the wall.

I was dreading having to separate them, but they were taken in by a Baker and his wife, though they had four of their own, and a baby. Insisted on taking them both, wouldn't hear of them being split up. I can't imagine how they will all fit into that tiny cottage. They said they would manage, the more the merrier. Beautiful smile she had, the mother. Those boys just looked at her, and you could tell it was love at first sight.

Were you born there? Is that further up the Valley? This is not a pretty place is it, no offence, the slag heaps and the pithead, grim rows of cottages. When you look up at the hills it's a different matter, must be beautiful on a clear day. I'd have loved a hike up there, but there's only this one train back.

Would you like a sandwich? Jam, so kind of that Post Mistress in the shop. Only charged me fourpence. Bramble jam. Delicious. Adore the smell of fresh baked bread, don't you?

I wish I could have stayed longer, I particularly wanted to find out about the children the headmaster brought here, last winter. One especially. Susan she was called. Sad story. She and her mother were the only survivors when their house in Wilmot Street was hit, the others hadn't made it to the shelter in time. Tragic. She wasn't in my class, no, but I used to keep an eye on her around the school. She wasn't strong, skinny little thing, wispy hair in pigtails, always a runny nose. Puff of wind would blow her over. Clever child, sharp as a tack at arithmetic. I hoped to be able to tell her mother I'd seen her. Those parents back in London wait and watch for letters that rarely come. I expect she's fine, the girl.

I'd like to launder your poor hanky and return it, if you don't mind giving me your address. Where are you doing your training? Barts? One of the best. The hostel for you tonight, is it? Too much for one day. They moved out to St Albans for the duration, didn't they, another long trip for you tomorrow. Very different to your country life, you'll find it. Watch out for those young Doctors – cheek of the devil, some of them – pretty girl like you!

DEFINING NAUGHTY.

1940

It's dark here on the landing, but they said I have to stand here and think it over. I'm not sure how to do that. This is creepy, this house, no one here but them and me. I can hear the wind outside and the trees swishing, and funny noises from all those empty rooms upstairs. I bet there's wild animals out there too, like wolves and that. London don't sound like this, it's noisy and busy with people and buses and shops and lights and things. Can't sleep with this creaky quiet and the whooshy wind.

I'm a bit worried at the moment though, 'cos my mum said I had to make sure I could lay hands on my gas mask at all times. I know where it is; they hung it on the nail by the back door, through the kitchen where they are now, by the range, having supper. I'd like some supper.
She's looking round the kitchen door.
'I hope you are standing still,' she shouts up.
'Yes, I am' I say, but I'm not, I'm bending my legs one by one, and wriggling my toes. I'm achey all over.

We went to Church today. Cor, it was posh! I had to wear my wellingtons though, cos the soles are coming off my boots. More money, him and her said. My feet were freezing wiv that stone floor. It was nice though, in the Church, the singing and that, and the coloured windows and the big Organ playing music. Afterwards everyone stood outside talking for ages, then this tall old woman with a long grey fur coat, definitely a dead wolf I reckon, probably shot it herself, came and patted me on the head, quite hard as it happens. 'So, this is your little evacuee, is it?' breathing her plummy winey breath on me. On her bony hand were rings wiv diamonds and emeralds and all jewels sparkling in the light. I couldn't help it, but I said 'Gawd blimey, love a duck, look at them rocks! You must be worth a bob or two!' She shot backwards, like I'd burnt her. I didn't mean nuffink rude; it's the truth, perhaps I should have said Mrs Madam, or your Highness or something.

Later on, when we got back here to Creepy Mansions, they said, didn't I know that blaspheming was very naughty, as was impertinence to one's elders and betters? I said no, I didn't. Well, I didn't know what I'd blasphemed, or how I'd done the other thing, I'm only six, don't know everything yet.

So, then he smacked my legs with his walking cane and said I had to stand up here and think it over. Well, I've tried to, but I don't know what to do next. I really need the lavvy.

My mum said I'd be safer away from the bombing in London. I don't feel very safe. It's dark now, outside, and up those stairs.

ROOM.

1940

'Room? we'll make room; the more the merrier, eh Dad?' says this round lady standing in the doorway, with all warm light behind her. She looked at me and my bruvver, and she smiled this big smile at us. 'Split 'em up? No that wouldn't be right, peas in a pod they are.'

Some other kids' faces appeared round the door, and one round her skirt.
The Welfare woman who brought us from the train looked happy.
'Well, if you're sure you've the room...'
It was getting dark; nobody in the village had wanted two of us, this was the last try, this house. We only had our jerseys, no coats, we was shivering.
'Let's get you inside,' said the Round Lady, so we picked up our attaché cases and went in. The Welfare woman handed over our ration books, and was gone like a flash down the street. Our teacher stood across the road, and did a little wave. She looked sad.

The inside was a big cosy kitchen, with a blazing fire in the grate, and a lovely smell of hot bread. Our mouths watered. It was a long time since our jam sandwiches on the train.
Round the table were some kids, and one in a baby chair. Our eyes nearly popped out at the sight of two big crusty loaves on the table and a big pot of something steaming in the middle.
The man pulled up two stools for us. 'Wash your hands in the sink, first, boys, and then we'll tuck in. Now then, who's who?

Usually when people asked us this, I'd say, cos my bruvver doesn't like talking much,
'He's Barry, and I'm not,' then we'd fall about laughing, but I thought I'd better do it right this time.
'He's Barry, and I'm Bobby. We're 'dentical twins.'
In the pot was a stew with lots of potatoes in, and we had big slices of bread to mop up with. We looked at each other, we always knew what the other one was thinking. Wherever

this Wales is, it must be next door to Heaven, cos we hadn't died!

When it was bedtime, we was embarrassed cos we had no pyjamas, just our vests and pants to sleep in. The round lady said not to worry, she'd sort it out tomorrow, and we'd have to top and tail on the camp bed tonight, and she'd sort that out too. She said to call her Aunty Gwen, and the man Uncle Dafydd. They don't half talk funny, but it's nice, like they're singing all the time. The other kids are real shy of us, we're too tired to worry. We're in a little room with the two other boys. The lavvy is out in the yard, and there's a bucket on the landing for night time emergencies. Just like home.

Aunty Gwen had washed the baby in the kitchen sink, like mum did with our baby Mary. After the bath the baby was all smiley and sleepy, ready for her cot. We thought about our mum and our baby, at home in London, and tried not to be sad, or think about the bombs.

We start early, said Aunty Gwen, Uncle Dafydd gets the first batch of loaves in the ovens next door in the shop, about five in the morning, so don't worry if you hear him banging about. He's not the quietest.

Me and Barry looked at each other as she tucked an eiderdown over us, we'd landed in a Baker's house. We fell asleep dreaming of warm crusty slices dripping with knobs of yellow butter.

1941

I think we've been here ages now, our trousers don't fit any more, so Aunty Gwen got some more from the Jumble Sale at the Chapel for us. We have to do lots to help the girls in the bakery cleaning things, cos they wash themselves better, says Uncle Dafydd, laughing. Us boys have to do the bread deliveries before School. Me and Barry get the bike, we go the furthest out to the Miners cottages by the pithead. Bit creepy out there. Nothing green. Big grey mountains of something called slag behind the houses.

Barry sits on the crossbar balancing the bread basket on the way out, and then we swop for the trip back. I'm stronger than him, cos I was born first, mum says. We miss her, but we don't have time to think about it. We all help with the vegetable garden too; we like that, we didn't have a garden in London. Before Dad went off to the war, he got some old beer barrels from the Birdcage Pub, down Columbia Road, and put them out the back in the yard and planted potatoes in them. So me and Barry know all about growing potatoes.

Something lovely happened. We got a letter from Mum! In the envelope was a picture of her and baby Mary by our front door, that Uncle Ted had taken with his Box Brownie. It made us happy. Baby Mary looks so big now, mum says she's got teeth and can eat some real food. And Mum's had a postcard from Dad, from a country called Egypt. That's where there's pyramids, I seen em in a book at school. I hope Dad and his friends are sleeping inside them, they'll be safe from the bombs in there.

We want to write her a letter, and we don't have paper, so we might ask our teacher. School's nice, we do lots of singing in their special language. We just make the noises. One time we sang baa baa black sheep and got the ruler from Mr Jones, so maybe we won't ask him.

We want to tell her all the lovely things Aunty Gwen makes with leftover bread – bread pudding with dried plums in, hot bread and butter pudding with sultanas or bramble jam, fried bread with an egg on top, and after the bathing in the scullery on Sunday nights, a bowl of hot bread and milk with honey on. It made us think about baby Mary now she's got teeth and wonder if she gets enough to eat.

I think it was Barry's idea first. We was taking a dozen loaves out to the Big House one Saturday, when Barry, balancing the basket on the crossbar, said,
'Ere, there's thirteen loaves. A dozen's twelve, innit?'

'Yep' I stopped pedalling, and got off and we counted them twice, to make sure. Thirteen it was.

'That's funny.' He looked at me hard. I could see he was thinking.

'How about we save number thirteen for Mum, hide it til we go home?'

And that's how it started.

Every time there was thirteen, we'd take one. There was an old empty pigsty up by the back of the shop, we hid them loaves in there, in a sack. It made us feel really happy to see the sack getting fatter, and we thought of Baby Mary getting fatter, like this baby here, who's got round cheeks and legs with folds.

But we wasn't expecting what happened next. It was Sunday night, we was all round the fire after bathing, with our bowls of hot supper, listening to 'Journey into Space' on the radio, when Uncle Dafydd says,

'We'll have to get that pigsty set up tomorrow, boys, the piglets will be coming in the afternoon. Taffy'll bring some straw and feed down.'

The girls squealed, with excitement. They wanted to play with the baby pigs, the boys were shouting oink oink, BACON! Me and Barry stopped breathing, spoons halfway to our mouths. We were going to have to do something quick smart. Uncle Dafydd would find the loaves and we'd be in big strife. We knew what happened to people who took what wasn't theirs to take.

Before Dad went off to do the War, he took us up Bethnal Green Police Station, and made us look down at the dark windows down below pavement level, the ones with bars on. We couldn't see in.

'Them's the dungeons, boys, where they put thieves and criminals.' He looked very serious.

'You keep out of trouble, you two, and ask if you want somethin.'

We nodded. We knew what dungeons were like, we'd been to the Tower. We'd been down the stone stairs to the underneath. We'd seen the chains on the wall. We'd smelt that cold dead smell.

Now we'd done something so bad we could get put in the dungeon, even if what we'd done was for our mum and our little sister.

Uncle Dafydd always locked up at night and took the keys to bed with him. We knew we had to move the bread, sharpish. We had to stay awake til the other kids were sparko, and we could hear Uncle Dafydd snoring in his bed; then we crept down to the scullery, climbed on the sink and got out the window, ran across the yard to the pigsty, and pulled the sack out. The loaves tumbled out. In the moonlight we could see they weren't bread colour anymore, they were green and black, and hard as rocks.

Uncle Dafydd's voice boomed out behind us, and we jumped out of our skins.

'Now then, boys, what are you at here then?' Barry started crying, without making a noise.

'Please don't put us in prison' I begged, 'We're so sorry.'

He looked at the scattered loaves, shaking his head, took us by the arms and into the kitchen.

'Aunt Gwen heard you, thought it was a burglar, sent me out in my nightshirt. Now tell me what this is all about? You hungry?'

'There was thirteen,' I said, 'not a dozen, we thought it was a mistake and no-one needed the extra. We wanted to save them for our mum, when we go home,' I hiccupped it all out. Barry couldn't talk at all.

What a shock, we got when Uncle Dafydd chuckled.

'Silly boys, thirteen is a Baker's dozen, that's what we call it.'

He packed us off to bed then, but we didn't sleep much. We were waiting for the knock on the door, and Dai the Policeman come to take us away.

Uncle Dafydd was very stern in the morning, and gave us a talking to about stealing. But then he said,

'Long time before you go home, boys. Here's what we'll do. Aunty Gwen's idea. I'll make a parcel for your mum, with a bag of bread flour, and some yeast, and we'll put it on the train to London, eh? How will that do?

We couldn't speak then, just looked at him. Barry's eyes were big and shiny, and I expect mine were too.

This Wales was not just a heaven but it's got angels without wings in it too.

DIARY.

1941

This old diary was in the bottom of the cupboard in my bedroom, mum, with a pencil inside that has a little gold tassel on the end. There are only a few pages written on, very scribbly writing that's hard to read. There's a name in the front; Susan Jacobs, 10 Quilter Street. That's just up the road from us in Bethnal Green, where we lived before the bombs came.

I know I shouldn't be looking in someone's diary, but there isn't a Susan here, and I think maybe she wouldn't mind if I use some paper from it to write to you. I had a pencil in my satchel when me and Billy got on the train at Liverpool Street, and somehow, I lost it. I'll try and get a stamp and an envelope (I can't ask Them). That kind lady in the Post Office might help me, she seems to like us kids. Sometimes she gives me a yesterday's bun when I take the eggs down. They talk funny here, mum, like a singing, it took a while to get used to it, and they have a whole secret language that they change into, when they don't want you to know what they're on about.

I read a bit of Susan's scribbly writing. She says she's missing her mum and that she's cold, and how it never stops raining, and how hard it is to get the coal in from the shed. I do that too, but I'm strong from helping dad on the stall down the market. Potatoes are as heavy as coal. I don't think Susan was as old as me, I'm nearly thirteen, true what she says about the rain though. They've just had to get me more boots, my feet didn't go in the old ones any more, and they leaked so I'd pinch some of the paper meant for the fire to soak up the squelch. Did they moan about that!

Are you alright, mum? I'm so sorry that I can't look after Billy like I promised; he went with different people to the big house outside the Village. I don't think they wanted a child at all, especially a skinny little boy like Billy, but the Welfare People made them have one, and he was the last one left. He was very brave, mum. Didn't cry. On the outside, anyway.

I see him on Sundays in the Church, we all have to go; he tries not to look at me because we're not allowed to talk. His people get cross. It's all very serious, and the Minister shouts a lot about Hell and Fire and Sins. In the kneeling bits I sometimes nod off, I'm so tired, and She elbows me to wake me up. Alright for her, she hasn't been up since 6, doing the fires, feeding the chickens and goats, getting breakfast ready, peeling the spuds and everything. I'm not moaning really, I do alright for food, I'm not a skinny minny anymore, like I was in London – getting quite chubby. She's not mean with my food, just words. Breakfast is always lovely porridge, made with goats' milk.

Sunday is the best day though, because They go and have a lie down after their dinner and I'm left to myself. I go out up the track behind the village, so no one sees me, to the big house, where Billy is. I see him through the window. Often, he's standing reading aloud to them from a great big book that looks like a Bible. He seems to make a lot of mistakes. Then the Man pokes him with his walking stick, which ain't fair – Billy's only seven, it's hard to read all that Exodus and stuff. If he sees me, he asks to go out to the Lav, and I'll meet him there and give him hugs to make up for the ones you can't give him. Sometimes I bring him a hardboiled egg, but I have to be a bit clever, cos she counts them.

Billy goes to school, I don't. They say work is all the education I need at my age.

I just looked at a bit more of Susan's spider writing. She says she's so homesick she can't eat, and her throat is so sore, she can't swallow. Then they get cross cos the food is wasted. I wonder where she went. There's some clothes in the cupboard that must have been hers, two jumpers and a coat. Too small for me, but it's cold up here, and I wrap them round me in bed at night, then put them back in the morning so no one knows. She says her head hurts and she wishes she was back in the East End, even with the bombs. I know what she means. All that lovely London, and neighbours looking out for each other, and the number eight taking you up west for a mooch around Oxford Street on a Saturday afternoon with you, mum. Sometimes a Sixpence to spend if it was a good week for dad.

Washing day tomorrow. Don't mind that that, cos it's all warm and steamy in the scullery; it's the mangling bit that's hard. Out in the yard, I do it, the cold and wet makes my hands sting. They'll have to get me some bigger clothes soon, the things I came with hardly go on now. I hope they notice. You'd hardly know me, mum, I'm going up like a lamppost!

I like doing the chickens, though, I have to feed them, and clean their house, and shut them in at night. It's cosy in their shed. Sometimes I'll crouch in there for a bit, with that nice straw smell, when they're settling down to roost and it's almost dark. They sort of purr at each other. And fidget and push for the best place on the perch. Sometimes I copy their chicken noises, and they fix me with a mean beady stare.

Sometimes I go up to the shed if She's gone out, and it's only Him in the house. Just lately he's taken to pinching my cheek or arm, and saying 'peaches and cream, peaches and cream' through his brown teeth, with his smelly breath. I'm wise to him, mum, don't worry, I helped me dad on the stall, remember? He could spot those handy andys, as he called em, a mile off. 'Don't turn your back on that one, chick,' he'd say. I don't know why I shouldn't, but I go up the shed out the way, til She gets back.

It's freezing up here in my room. It's Easter today, soon be Spring. If they get Spring here! I've got Susan's coat round my legs. I'm trying not to be nosy reading her diary, and wondering where she went. I keep thinking about her. She sounds so unhappy. The last bits of writing are really wobbly. She says her eyes hurt, and her chest, and she can't stop coughing. Scared she says. Wants to be back home, even with the bombs.

So do I. Me and Billy, all of us together again. I'm trying to be tough. It gets harder. I wonder why Susan didn't take her diary, when she left? People always take their diaries.

Can you come and fetch us mum? Billy's got a cough, all raspy, I hear him in Church, though he tries hard to stop.

INVITATION.

1942

Dear Mrs Johnson,

            I hope you don't mind me taking the liberty of writing to you. There are things I think you ought to know about your children. I am Post Mistress and have the little shop here in Hurwyn, where they are billeted as you know. Your girl brings the eggs from the Parry place, I see her regular like. She wanted to send you a postcard, so I let her have one, and a stamp, she hasn't any money of her own, (that's twopence for the stamp and sixpence for the card, by the way) and I took down the address off it.

I'm not interfering, no, but I do like to keep an eye on these evacuee children. Poor little scraps some of them are, and not every foster home is as good as it might be. Naming no names, mind you.

The reason I'm writing, is that I've got your boy Billy here with me. The people at the big house said they couldn't keep him, not with that cough, and needing nursing. Couldn't get the coal in or do his jobs. I don't know if the Welfare people have told you they moved him? Asked if I'd take him in, well, couldn't say no, could I?

I never had children, never carried full term, see. A pity it was, for me and my Dai (God rest him), but you have to make the best of it don't you?

Your boy, he's been here a fortnight already, and picking up now, he is. Doctor's been three times, and given him some strong medicine, (two bob it was), and now he needs rest and good feeding he says. I didn't like to say I didn't think they fed him properly up at the Minister's house. Funny. They're not short.

I'm making a rabbit stew, like I used to make for Dai. I get the rabbits cheap off Ewan, and I don't ask where he gets them. Your Billy he loves my stew, and a bit of Barabrith cake; haven't made that for a long while either. Doctor says he can get out of bed tomorrow, and come downstairs for a bit. Have a change of scene. Looking quite bright he is now, got these shiny brown eyes and those little freckles across his nose - but you know that already. Be giving me cheek, before long, I don't doubt.

Your big girl will be down tomorrow with the eggs, she'll pop in to see him. She worries about him. Lovely girl she is. I shall tell her I'm writing to ask you to visit, but to keep it quiet, for now. Funny people those Parrys. She's tough, never complains, works hard. I need to say something on her behalf, though, something a bit personal. She's growing up, see and well, she needs a brassiere. Wondered if you could post some, or bring them if you come?
That Parry, he looks at her you know, I'm not the only one to notice. She needs a mother's talk if you get my meaning, not my place to do that. She's fourteen, going to be a looker, you can tell.

Reminds me of myself at that age. Innocent as the day I was. Easy to get into trouble, when you don't know anything? Only one kind of trouble, isn't there, I should know.

They took the baby away, I didn't even know what was happening, I thought I was dying. All that blood. Had him in the barn, a little boy, with big brown eyes. I never saw him again, and I never got in the family way again when me and Dai were married. He said he didn't mind, we were happy. He'd have loved a son, he would.

There I've written it down. It was never talked about at home, ever. Like that baby never existed. Why am I telling you? I don't know what's come over me. Your girl, the way she talks about you, how kind you are to everyone, and always got time to listen, what a loving mother you are. I could have been a mother like that given a chance. Maybe having your lad here has made me think about that baby again. Like a skinny little rabbit, he was. Like your Billy when he first arrived.

He's doing fine now, don't worry. Be helping me in the shop before long.

They never sent me up the Dairy again for the cream. That boy up there. The one who... Think they sent him off to the army. No one ever said.

So I'm inviting you to come and stay, if you can get leave from the Munitions factory, you can stop here, share with Billy. I'll only ask you for half a crown, if you would want hot dinners at night.

Yours truly, Gwyneth Evans.

SEARCHING.

1943

London

Dear Teacher,

　　I apologise for not knowing your name, but I am trying to find my Susan, and I think she must have been to your School in the village. The authorities have been no help, and can't tell me where she is, only where she was left. That was the Parry farm, they said.

I have been ill, after an operation for my appendix, which went badly, and I had to go for convalescence for six months, out in the country. I am better now, and living with my sister in Enfield, and I need to find my girl.

Her name is Susan Jacobs, she will be ten now, and she has fair hair, and grey eyes, and is small for her age. She's a clever girl, but very shy about speaking up for herself. Can you help me?

Yours sincerely,

Mrs Sarah Jacobs.

Hurwyn

Dear Mrs Jacobs,

　　Thank you for your letter, and I am sorry to hear of your illness, and sorrier still to say that your daughter has not been a pupil at my School. I have checked my registers thoroughly, and can find no mention of a Susan Jacobs.

I will telephone the Welfare People tomorrow from the Post Office and try to ascertain your daughter's whereabouts.

Please try to contain your anxiety; If Susan is here, we will locate her.

Yours sincerely,

Aled Davies.

London

Dear Mr Davies,

       I am so sorry to put you to this trouble. Thank you so much for your kindness. I would be on the first train to Wales, but I was given a War Office appointment, which is top secret, so I can't tell you anything. My old Headmistress at Spital Square Grammar recommended me, with my maths abilities. I was supposed to go to university, but I met my Ted, and our little Susan came along. Ted was killed when she was a baby, there's only me and her Nanna, I must find her. She doesn't even know our house was bombed, or about her cat Sooty.

  Miss Menzies (my headmistress) had friends in high places, if you know what I mean, and she put me forward for this posting. It's vital work, but I will put in for some compassionate leave.

       Yours with thanks,

       Sarah Jacobs.

Hurwyn

Dear Mrs Jacobs,

       I have made enquiries concerning Susan of the Post Mistress here, and of my pupils, and have been assured that Susan was at the Parry Farm, before the girl Carol; who, like Susan, is not permitted to attend school either. Most irregular, the evacuee children are obliged to attend.

  I plan to cycle out to the farm on Saturday, and speak to Mr Parry, and ascertain your daughter's whereabouts. You are causing me no nuisance; I am happy to help.

       Yours sincerely,

       Aled Davies.

Dear Mrs Jacobs,

I have at last some answers for you, though not all you would require. Mr and Mrs Parry at the Farm were rather defensive about telling me anything at first, until it became clear that I was not to be thwarted, and they would be getting into hot water if they were not compliant.

They eventually told me that Susan had become so sickly, and unable to do her chores, that they were obliged to send for Dr Hughes; who removed her at once and took her to the cottage hospital in Merthyr. I have spoken to Dr Hughes, he has his Surgery here three times a week, and he remembered well the case. He thought that your daughter probably had tuberculosis. He does not know any more; such a busy man.

The Hospital will be my next point of inquiry. Please bear up. We will find her.

Yours

Aled Davies

London

Dear Aled,

I am so grateful to you. You must be a wonderful person to help a stranger like this. I have applied for some compassionate leave to come to Wales.

With thanks,

Sarah

Hurwyn

Dear Sarah,

      Forgive the delay in an answer, I have at last some more definite news for you.

I have received a reply from the Hospital at Merthyr, who assured me that Susan is safe and well. She had been taken from there to a TB hospital down the valley, where she was for some months, in the country air, getting her cure. From thence to a Convalescence Unit. Only three weeks ago she was transferred to a Foster Home, where she is thriving, I am told. Letters had been sent to your address in London, but of course could not be delivered as you had been bombed out.

Susan has been told that you will be coming soon. She is very excited and is writing you a letter which will come here as she has not been given an address.

I am happy to help you. The opportunity for becoming a father has not been my privilege yet in life, but I am optimistic. The children in my care at School are as valued as my own would be.

When the letter comes, may I open it, so that you do not have to wait any longer, and the letter will not go astray in London. Might I telephone you somewhere? Forgive me if this is too much intrusion.

        With best wishes,

          Aled.

SARAH.

1942

I can hardly believe I am on the train at last! We left Paddington two hours ago, and I'm loving watching the country roll by, I've only seen these places on the films. Hurry up hurry up, I say to the wheels, bring me to Hurwyn.

Aled, the Schoolmaster is going to meet me at the station with his brother's car, and I will stay with the brother and his wife Aled being a bachelor, said it wouldn't be proper for me to lodge with him; there'd be talk.

He had such a lovely voice on the phone, when he read me Susan's little letter. I wonder what he's like? I couldn't wait any longer to hear what she said. He posted it on after to my sister's house and I've got it here safe in my bag. I have to keep re reading it, though I know it by heart now. It was like Christmas. I'm afraid I cried. The relief of knowing she is safe. If it hadn't been for the kindness of this stranger, I might never have found her. Makes me think there must be lots of children who 've lost their families because of this beastly war! If I could take them all home, I would.

I hope Aled will recognise me, I told him I'll be wearing a red coat, with a velvet collar, and I've got sort of dark fair hair, if you know what I mean. I was blond like Susan when I was a child. This coat is quite smart, I think, even though I picked it up in the market. Fits well. I wonder if I'll know who he is? Couldn't tell how old from his voice. Soon as I hear that voice again, I'll know it's him.

I keep opening my bag, and holding her letter. To make it real and not a dream. I think I can say it by heart now; I've read it so many times.

Dear mummy,

 I am so happy you are comin to see me at last. I thought you wood never find me again. I thought I was a norfan, wen I was at the hospital. The people I stay with are very kind and Mrs Loid makes lovely dinners with lovely gravy. The school is nice, and we do Nature walks outside in the woods. We found a Stag Beetle. Some children screemed but I didn't.
 Please bring me some hair slides, if you can and my small doll.
 I hope you will no who I am. I got tall.

  With lots of love

  Your Susan xxxxxx

 I have to dry my eyes again – how am I going to tell her that her small doll, her big doll, all her precious things were lost in the bombing? She will be so upset. If I'd had some spare money, I could have got a little doll; but it wouldn't be her Candy. The hair slides I got will make her happy, I hope.

They've lit me a fire in this little bedroom over the kitchen. I was shivery and exhausted when we finally arrived. There's a woollen knitted blanket over the top of my bed, and they gave me a stone hot water bottle for my feet. Very cosy. Outside on the hill I can hear the sheep; they make a lot more noises than just a baa. Surprise to a city girl like me! They seem to have coughs! Don't know how you'd give a sheep linctus - you'd have to catch one first! I'm making myself giggle at the thought.

 We had a wonderful supper with a mutton stew and potatoes, cooked in the Aga, and bread with a whole week's ration of butter each! Real butter! They are so kind. I'm full to bursting and warm right through. So happy to be here at last.

Aled knew me straight away at the station. He is very tall, looks very serious, and has floppy brown hair. He might be forty, hard to tell, then you look in his face and eyes and see he is younger than he seems, and has this twinkle.

He gave me a package. It's here on my lap. The T.B. Hospital sent it; it's full of the letters that Susan wrote to me when she was ill. I'm going to read them, though my fingers are shaking, before we go to see her tomorrow. My precious girl. After Ted died in the Tram accident, there's only been me and her Nanna. She doesn't remember him at all, she was so little. Here goes.

DEAR MUM.

Merthyr Tydfil Hospital

June

Dear Mum,

      I think I've been in the Hospital a long time. Doctor said I had T.B and newmonia, and I am a lucky girl becos I am getting better. He sent you a letter, but you did not come. When can you come?

It was very cold on the Farm, when I was ill. The Doctor from the village took me to the Hospital in his big car. I wish I could remember. Mum, I said my prayers for you to come.

Is Sooty orlright? Does he miss me? I want to see him so bad, and cuddle him in my bed. He is the best cat.

I will be able to go in the Playroom with the other kids, Nurse said, if I eat all my dinners. I try but sometimes I am so sad, I cant swallow. Even on jelly day. Please come soon.

      With best love,

      Susan. Xxxxxxxxxxxxx

Greenfield Sanatorium

August

Dear Mum,

      I am in another place, where we get con-val-esince. I don't think we had it yet. We do have malt on a spoon, it's lovely, but some kids make faces and pretend to be sick.

We do lessons outside under the trees in the garden, that is nice. I'm getting brown legs. Some kids got sunburns. We do P.T in the garden, to mend our lungs.

It was a lucky day yesterday. We went to the Village shop and in the shop were lots of jars of sweets all colors. We all had a threepenny bit to spend from the Welfare lady. I got tuppence - worth of sherbet lemons, and four blackjacks for a penny. It was hard to choose.

There is visiting day on Sunday for your family. Please can you come? I think I am still in Wales. I can find out the place for you.

I miss you and Sooty.

Your loving daughter Susan xxxxx

Greenfield Sanatorium

November

Dear Mum,

There was a gale. It rained and rained, and we have to stay indoors now. We have our lessons indoors. The Caretaker man lites a fire in the classroom. That is nice. I am very well, my legs are getting fatter. I hope you are very well too.

The Travelling Pictures came, and we saw Charlie Chaplin A Dog's life. It was funny.

Is my Nanna orlright? I had a dream about her. She was cold in the street and the bombs were falling round her.

We are giving a play for Christmas. It is the story of Baby Jesus being born. I think I will be Angel Gabriel, who is the Boss of the Angels. I have to say Lo the Child is born. Go at once to the stable by the Inn. I say it to the shepherds. One kid said we could catch a real sheep from the field and take it on the stage. We all started laughing. Miss Jones got very cross and stopped the practice.

Do you think you mite come to watch us do the Play? The Doctor comes to see us tomorrow. I will ask him.

Love from your Susan xxxx

Greenfield Sanatorium

Dear Mum,

     I wish I could show you my work today, I got two gold stars. We did fractions, I like that a lot and that was one gold star. Then I wrote a story about Sooty when he was a kitten and he fell in the bath with me and started to swim and when he climbed the curtain and could not get down and you climbed up to get him and he jumped down before you could get him. I read it to the class and Miss Jones and they all laughed. So that was my other gold star.

     Your loving daughter Susan xxxxxx

Rose Cottage

February

Dear Mum,

     I am in a new place now, in a house with a family. It is a foster house. I am all better from TB! Doctor said I am very well! There is another girl here like me who had bad TB, she is called Pat. We made friends. Gess what, she lives round the corner of Hackney Road, and goes to Teesdale Juniors. She has three brothers, and gess what, they all go down Columbia Road Market on Sunday morning to the broken biscit man and the shellfish man and get winkles for tea like us! She said she's the best at getting the winkle out of the shell on the pin without breaking it. Better than her brothers.

  I got sad thinking about Sunday tea by the fire, brown bread and butter and picking the winkles out. Uncle Mac on the radio and Larry the Lamb.

  Can Pat come to tea when we all go home? She is nice. She gave me a ribbin for my hair.

Please come soon Mum, Mrs Loid said your War Work is very imp-or-tant. They will try to get a letter to you.

Bye Bye for now.

Your loving Susan. xxxx

HERE BE DRAGONS.

1944

Them London kids. I thought I'd be glad when they went away, but I'm not; I'm all wobbly inside. They're packing their cases upstairs now, ready for tomorrow and the journey. I can hear the drawers opening and shutting - bang bang.

Me Mam is helping them. When she went up, she looked as though she might cry; gives me a funny feeling. I've got to watch our littlest, she's asleep in the pram outside the front door. She's three now, and she can undo her straps if she wakes up. She was a baby when them kids came.

I was so jealous. I thought what about us? No room for more kids here, we got enough. But me Mam and Da said we should be kind, cos we were saving them from Hitler, and they'd had to leave their own Mam and Da behind.

We didn't talk to them for ages, cos we couldn't understand what they said, in their London talk, and they couldn't understand us either. One of them wet the bed too, and my brother used to whisper baby needs a nappy, until me Da heard him and went real wild.

We had to take them to School with us, and we weren't nice to them in the playground. Someone said if they're from London they must have fleas; everyone there has them, he said. Their vacuee had them, and they all had to have paraffin on their heads till the fleas died, so we'd shout call Nitty Nora, call Nitty Nora with her scratchy comb and we'd chase them twins into the lavvies in the playground and not let them out until lesson time. They never said nuthin though.

We weren't nice. I feel bad about that now. The thing was we thought Mam was using up all her love on them, and wouldn't have enough left for us. Me and my sister used to hear her singing them to sleep, that song about God and Angels watching you all through the night, and I know she will be stroking their hair, the way she does ours, and I feel all empty inside cos she isn't doing it to me and I can't say anything cos their own mam isn't here to do it. One night me and my sister cried when she came to say goodnight, and said did she love them twins more than us, and she just laughed and cuddled us up. She said love is like a piece of elastic, the more you stretch it, the more there is. We didn't really understand, but it did make us feel a little bit better.

We did some horrible things to them at first, put salt in their porridge when they weren't looking, and worms in their beds, and I hid their shoes in the coal shed one time so they were late for school, but oh no that wasn't the worst, this was the worst.

It was all me, I'm the eldest, I'm eleven, my brothers are ten and eight. I thought if we could just get rid of them, everything would be normal again, and we wouldn't have to share our Mam anymore. So I said to the others let's pretend we're going to show them where the Welsh Dragon lives, that'll scare them. We'll tell them it eats children who can't speak Welsh, and then they'll cry to go home.

My brothers and my little sister looked worried. Where's it live then our Carys? Is it red, like on the flag?

It's not real you dafties, we're just pretending!

So we kidded them twins on, and they believed me, and we took them up out the village, past the slag heaps to one of the old Mine Shafts, which wasn't used any more cos it was dangerous. We were absolutely not sposed to go up there.

So we walked inside real slow, looking down into the dark tunnel, where you can't see the bottom, and I shouted down into it, in Welsh, to the Dragon, come out and eat these silly kids who think you're real; and then in English give us a sign O mighty Welsh Dragon and we're all peering and listening when there's this sudden big rumbling and thundering right down underground. And yellow smoke comes shooting out in a cloud, and the ground sort of cracked under our feet and the little ones scream the dragon, the dragon…

Well, did we run! Never so fast in all my life, back down past the slag, slipping and sliding in the grey dust. My little sister fell over and Barry picked her up and put her on his shoulder, I liked him then, and we ran down the street, past the shop, into the alley by the Church. We couldn't breathe hardly and my ribs hurt and we had grey dust up our legs and all over our shoes, that we'd have to get off before we went home, or we'd be in strife.

Gavin the Post came by in his van and stopped at the end. He saw our trouble, and knew where we'd been, and gave us an old mail sack to clean up a bit with. Real kind. He touched the side of his nose with his finger and said mum's the word. I think he was smiling.

The thing was them twins never split on me and told our Mam how I'd tricked them and taken them and the little ones up the Pit, to see the Dragon that wasn't really there, so after that I decided they were ok and we'd stop being mean.

So we was all friends in the end. They were funny. Funny way of making jokes with words. they'd say, where's my titfer? Tit for tat, HAT, get it?

And let's have a butcher's. Took us ages to get that, they just kept laughing. Butcher's hook, LOOK! They said in the end. They think our Welsh is weird, well their London is crackers!

Now they are going home. Their Mam is here, she'll be sleeping downstairs on the Put-U-Up, she's nice, got curly hair like them. They'll get the train tomorrow, and all the other kids who stayed in the village, it's safe now in London, Mr Churchill says. Mam wants us all to go and wave them off; Da has given them cake, and jam and bacon and a big piece of cold mutton. I gave them a picture I drew of the dragon.

Mam says when the War is really over we can go and visit them, and see the Tower, and the dungeons and the chopping block and the Crown Jewels and wave to the King, and go on a red bus and everything. I hope they don't forget. Our teacher says we will all write letters to them, so they can't forget.

HAPPINESS.

1944

Mum says 'I'm so happy.' With her arms round both of us, squeezing us tight. My happy feels like a big bubble in my chest, all warm and swelling up, and spreading all through me. We're sitting on the Station platform, waiting for our train; I'm squashed between my mum and my sister on the wooden bench, with our bags and attaché cases tucked under our feet. The Station is really crowded. Lots of the other kids are going home today as well.

Home. Going home. To London. Safe now, mum says, the war is over, you can leave your gas mask off. I won't though, it's round my neck, where I can lay hands on it if I need to. Like mum and my teacher told me in the first place.

Mrs Evans in the Post office, she packed us up some egg sandwiches, and some Barabrith cake for the journey. They're wrapped up in greaseproof, in my sister's satchel. I can almost smell them, my mouth's watering already. Praps we'll get a nibble when we get on the train.

She had tears in her eyes, Mrs Evans, when we said goodbye. I hugged her tight round her apron, and she ruffled my hair with her hand. Everyone thinks she's such a dragon, but I think she's like an egg, all hard shell on the outside, with the soft bit hidden in the middle. Told me to be sure to write, and be good and do my jobs in the house like she taught me, and work hard at school, and to come back to visit one day; and then she ran out of words, and just hugged me back tight until it got embarrassing.

Mum says we can't go home to our old house, cos Baxendale Street got bombed, and where our house was is just debris now. That made me sad. We're going to stay in Aunty Lil's back bedroom til Dad gets back from the War. She's making us a bread pudding for tea tonight, and if she's got enough sterilised milk left we'll have custard with it.

Dad's coming back from the War. He's alright. Everyone thought he was shot, but they found him camping in a place called Burma. I'm not sure where that is, but it might have a jungle. Monkeys, snakes and tigers, I reckon.

The Boy Scouts used to go camping up Epping Forest; I saw them once before I was vacuated, packing all their tents and stuff on a handcart. They were big boys, got uniforms, and a whistle each, and they've all got a tin mug and a penknife tied on their belts wiv string. I'd like a penknife. I'd like to go camping, like the Scouts and my Dad.

We're going to have a prefab from the Council, mum says. It's a whole little house with walls that come already built. They bring it on a lorry and put it all together for you. We'll have our own toilet out the back, not sharing like before, and water in a tap with our own sink, and a copper to make the water hot; and a little garden with a fence. Praps I can have a dog. I miss Mrs Evans dog Bryn already and I bet he's looking for me. He's a black and white Collie dog, with soft fur and a long pink tongue. She let him sleep on my bed when I was ill and they brought me to her house. When I was better he was supposed to stay in the kitchen, but he used to creep up the stairs real quiet and get back on my bed again. It was nice. I think she knew, but she pretended she didn't, else she'd have to have told him off.

I'll ask Dad, when he gets home, if we could go down Club Row market and buy a puppy, they got everything down there, puppies and kittens, and birds and chickens. I'll tell him I know all about looking after dogs now.

'Here comes the train' says my sister. We can see a puff of smoke coming up the valley. My sister, she's so grown up now, she's like a lady. She still tweaks my nose though and tickles my ribs, like when I was a little kid. It's nice, but I pretend I hate it.

And here's the train, screeching brakes, doors banging open, everyone chattering and pushing to clamber in and get the best seats by the windows, whistle blowing, and we're off! We wave out of the window to no one in particular, goodbye, goodbye, to Wales, and sheep and village and Bryn, and Mrs Evans. Going home.

And the happy bubble inside me just gets bigger. I think I'll take my Gas Mask off now.

GOODBYES.

1943

Watch with me now; the last of them are leaving today, the children. There has been a steady procession down the hill from the Village to the Station. Only one train to Paddington today, the ten fifteen. There's a buzz in the air: the lucky ones who have had a parent or relative collect them are chattering like starlings, excited, racing ahead. Those without are being escorted by their Headmaster, who has come to take them back to London to foster homes, and one little chap to Barnado's. They are quieter, anxious, clutching their battered cases and bags, gas mask boxes still around their necks.

And all of them wondering what 'home' actually means now? They've seen the newsreels on the Travelling Pictures of their city; houses and whole streets gone, flattened by the bombs. They've seen the brave Civil Defence men pulling people out of the rubble, and quenching fires with giant snakes of hosepipe.

It is safe now, the Blitz is over, say the Government. Big Ben still chimes, Nelson still stands watch over his lions; the mighty dome of St Paul's shines high and proud. A miracle says the BBC when flames blazed all round it, that it survived.

Looking at them now, gathered on the platform, they look like different children to those that arrived three years ago, they are grown, strong legged, country cheeked, well fed (for the most part). They are all straining now for the first glimpse of the train coming down the line.

And here she is; the Great Western, her gleaming livery restored, having been painted matt black during the blitz years, a plume of white smoke from the chimney stack announcing her arrival. A brief expectant silence falls – then shouts of 'it's coming, it's coming', - the rumbling getting louder, the engine belching, pulling into the Station with a squeal of brakes.

A flurry of movement, last hugs and promises, scrambling into carriages with boxes and bags, slamming the doors, dropping the window strap, fighting for a space to lean out and shout, 'goodbye, goodbye, don't forget to write'.

The Guard shouts, 'MIND THE DOORS' with authority, blows his whistle, and waves his flag to the driver. The noise of the Engine drowns the last shouts, as it picks up speed, passing the end of the platform.

Gradually, those left behind begin to drift away. The hosts who have put their charges on the train trickle through the barrier: some briskly, job done; others reluctantly, as though they've left something important behind. A long time since the children arrived on the London train with their teacher, with white faces, tired limbs, and empty bellies.

Gwen, the Baker's wife, openly dabbing her eyes with a hanky, gathers her children close around her. Her big warm heart feels as if there is a hole in it now the twins have gone off on the train. She'd sent them off looking bonny, though, she says to herself. Grown out of every stitch they'd brought with them, nice round bodies on them. A job well done, taking care of them for their mother. Had a job to recognise 'em she'd said. The youngest two of her own cling to her skirt, worried they might be put on a train too.
'Just us for dinner now, my ducks,' she says.

The boys run on ahead, with long faces, pushing and shoving each other, pretending not to care. The eldest girl drags behind, looking back. She still carries a guilt about how horrid she had been to the twins, even though it had been alright in the end.

The Postmistress Gwyneth lingers, as though a part of her has left with Billy. And perhaps it has. The Collie dog pulls back on his lead, knowing things are not right, someone important is missing. Gwyneth hadn't gone onto the platform, she'd said goodbye outside and left Billy to his mother and sister, as was only correct. She can see the train growing smaller. She wonders how she can bear her empty home now. A plan begins to form in her head, and a hopeful little smile touches her mouth. There must be many children left with nobody of their own, maybe she'd be considered a good foster home – after all she had experience now. She would ask the Welfare Woman how to put her name down. They wouldn't be Billy, but maybe a nice Welsh girl, who would help in the shop after school?

The Parrys aren't here to wave either Carol or Susan off. No surprise there. Too much work to do, and no help. Parry, mucking out the goat shed, sucks at his loose tooth, and stamps his cold feet irritably. Have to do something about things, he thinks. They could apply for one of those Italian prisoners of war, maybe, from the Camp up the valley. Don't have to feed them, they get taken back at night and fed. He starts to sing 'Bread of Heaven' hoarsely. Doesn't notice that one of the goats is quietly and methodically chewing a hole in the waterproof he left over the stable door.

Mrs Parry is trying in vain to get the Rayburn fire in the kitchen to light. Carol always did this, it's a knack. Kept it in overnight too. She curses quietly, she hates this contraption, doesn't have the patience. 'As if I haven't enough to do' she mutters. There's a little burst of a red glow, and thinking she's beaten the stove this time she slams the vent shut, whereupon the glow splutters and fades. Even that sickly girl before Carol could manage to get it burning, she thinks to herself. All that gossip in the Village about that child. Wasn't our fault she got sick. She'd have to go down with the eggs herself now, face that nosey Gwyneth in the Post Office, some sort of saint, is she? Them down the Village think she is since she took that boy in. She opens the little glass door, stuffs more paper and damp wood inside, strikes a match again.

The Minister and his wife had come, to be seen to be there; but nobody had smiled or spoken to them, just the briefest of nods, from some. The Minister's wife looks sideways at her husband's stony profile, feeling the unspoken disapproval of the Villagers; a little finger of guilt creeping through her chest. Maybe she should have stood up to him, been kinder to the boy... But then she had seen the scars on her own husband's back, that had never been acknowledged by him, and that she'd never dared to ask about. If they'd had their own children, it might have been different. It seemed it was common knowledge how they had treated their evacuee; the Postmistress had seen to that.

That the truth will always out, is indeed a truth, as is clear in the Bible. 'Be sure your sins will find you out' says the cross stitched text that hangs on the wall of the Manse, carefully worked by the Minister's wife. It had struck fear into Billy's young heart every time he sat at the table for a meal; it was facing him, and he was never quite sure if he had done some sins he didn't know about.

Aled, the tall thin Schoolteacher, in his gabardine mac, stands alone at the last, at the end of the platform, watching the train wind down the track through the valley, until it is the size of a Matchbox toy. His mind was full of his last sight of Sarah, looking back at him over the shoulder of her red coat, holding her daughter's hand tightly as they boarded the train. Susan had stood on tiptoe and reached up to kiss his chin, which was all she could reach. Impulsively Sarah kissed him too, touching her warm cheek to his for a second.

Only the smallest column of smoke is visible now, as the train disappears behind the curve of the hill. An unfamiliar ache has begun inside Aled, as he turns to go.

She said she would come back. She said she would. And if she doesn't? the doubting voice says.

Well Boyo, you'll just have to go and find her then! He instructs himself. Take yourself by the scruff of the neck. He retrieves his bicycle from where it's propped outside the Ticket Office, and begins to whistle as he pedals away.

Dear Mum We
School again yesterday.
In the afternoon we
went shopping in the village
It was a lucky day
one shop of yesterday
sweets all day for our lesson
in Saturday we all
to the pictures to see
another wore "tight"
so enjoyed it... we have
look over we have
to have school indoors
Last night there was a gale
I'm feeling very
Well and hope you are in
good health too. I should
be very glad if you could
bring me paper and
envelopes.
and my little doll
Hoping to hear from

it is raining this morning
so we could not go out.
the doctor is coming
to see us tomorow
Rat that I send

We are very busy at
the moment getting
ready to a Nativity Play to
give school. The rest of the
like are going to give money
on the stage and Slave
x x x
love
x x x x
x x x x

I hope Tim ey
is cool note. He
hope

Mummy I am are very fresh
you have been
we much lessons
so I test
because to get
home. I hope
Dear
Well
3 0

ACKNOWLEDGEMENTS.

Firstly, I thank my daughter for her patience and tolerance in getting me to the stage of publication.

I thank Nikki Davies, my illustrator, who gave life to my voices.

I thank Sue H, for her assistance in planting my reluctant feet on the technology path.

I thank my cousin Georgina, for allowing the use of her invaluable letters.

ABOUT THE AUTHOR.

Chris Andrews was born in 1946, in Bethnal Green Hospital, London, (though almost on the 253 bus in Hackney Road)- the definitive Baby Boomer. She grew up in Baxendale Street in a Prefab, as her parents had lost their home during the Blitz. The family had very little, materially or financially, but didn't know it, as most people they knew were in the same boat. What she and her sister did have was love, full bellies, and a father who was always there with stories, books, paints, paper, clay, and the patience to allow them to create and explore, alongside an infinitely tolerant mother. Accompanied always by assorted animals and encouragement to grow flowers and food in the garden.

Chris was fortunate enough to gain a place at the Girls' Grammar School in the City, and receive food for her developing mind. She began to write poetry at about the age of twelve, which continued throughout her life, because she couldn't not; an idea and phrase would start in her head and might be months before turning into words on a page.

She sold some poems here and there, but never pursued it. Her personal life was complicated, and physical, with horses, dogs and children to be cared for.

She published articles and wrote reports during her working years whilst her literary life continued, with studying, courses and reading. She came to teaching late in life (her happy place) having qualified to teach in Adult Education. Poetry was still happening, though she had not explored the short story form until joining a Writer's Group on retirement. It was pure pleasure, being given a topic to write about, to twist any which way you wanted. Through this, she learnt to focus and discipline her writing; to mentally construct a story, instead of waiting for the non-existent Muse to descend.

And so began this series of voices of evacuee children, who tell their own stories.

www.ingramcontent.com/pod-product-compliance
Lightning Source LLC
Chambersburg PA
CBHW040714220426
43209CB00091B/1838